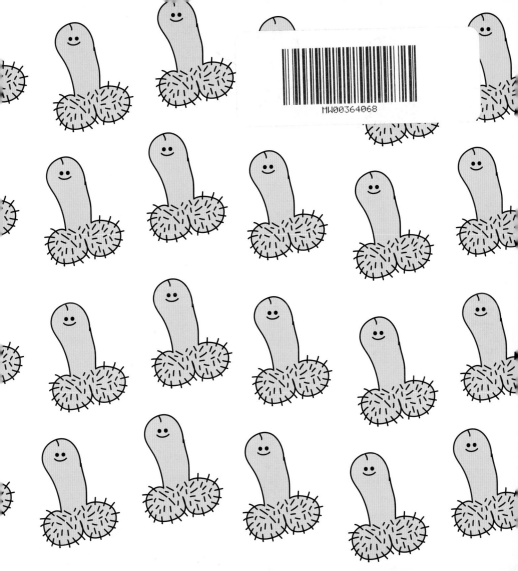

DICKTIONARY

223 Fun Words
for Penis!

By Todd Harris Goldman

RUNNING PRESS
PHILADELPHIA • LONDON

Printed in China

9 8 7 6 5 4 3 2 1
Digit on the right indicates the number of this printing

Library of Congress Control Number: 2009938623

ISBN 978-0-7624-3933-1

Designed and illustrated by Todd Harris Goldman
Edited by Greg Jones
Typography: ITC American Typewriter

Running Press Book Publishers
2300 Chestnut Street
Philadelphia, PA 19103-4371

Visit us on the web!
www.runningpress.com

Intro**DICK**tion

A rose by any other name would still be a rose. But a penis by any other name might be a "Kentucky Telescope," "Molten Mushroom," "Pump-Action Porridge Bazooka," or even "King Kong Schlong!"

Whether your member leans left or right, is smooth or shaggy, thick or thin, touches the floor or barely peeks through the barn door, it's still YOUR unit and it deserves a fun nickname!

That's where DICKtionary comes in handy (so to speak). Just like those popular baby-naming books—only rated R for raunchy—DICKtionary offers hours of fun while searching for the perfect handle (so to speak) for your little buddy.

So what are you waiting for? Keep turning the pages until you pick the perfect moniker. It's not so hard! (So to speak.)

#1 Admiral Winky

#2 Albino Cave Dweller

#3 Ankle Spanker

#4 Anteater

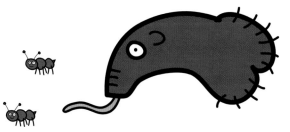

#5 Apple-Headed Monster

RARRRR!

#6 Bacon Bazooka

#7 Bald Eagle

#8 Bald-Headed Jesus

#11 Banana Boat

#12 Bat-n-Balls

#13 Bearded Beaver Burgler

#14 Beef Twinkie

#15 Big Jake the One-Eyed Snake

#16 Biscuit Inspector

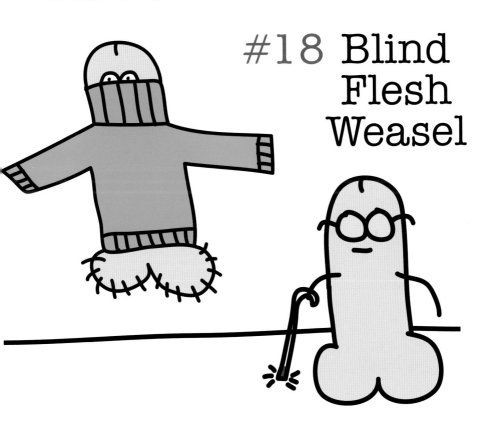

#19 Blow Pop

#20 Blue-Veined Junk Pumper

#21 Bob the Book Worm

#22 Bottle-Nosed Dolphin

#23 Bow-Legged Swamp Donkey

#24 Breakfast Burrito

#25 Bubba the Love Slug

#26 Bushwhacker

#27 Buster Hymen

#28 Camel Toe Jockey

#29 Captain Caveman

#30 Cervix Crusader

#31 Cherry Picker

#32 Chick Stick

#33 Chimney Sweeper

#34 Chowder Pumper

#35 Clam Diver

#36 Clit Tickler

#37 Cockasaurus Rex

#38 Colon Cowboy

#39 Cornhole Crusader

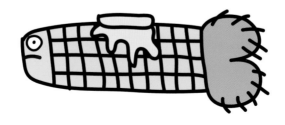

#40 Cream Master D

#41 Creamsicle

#42 Crotch Rocket

#43 Cum Pump

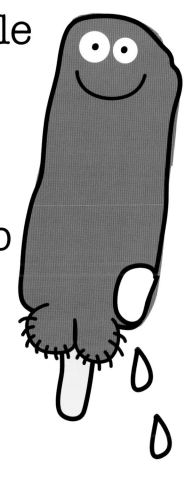

#44 Custard Cannon

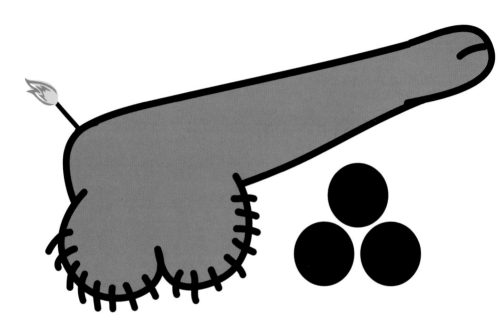

#45 Daddy Long Leg

#46 Cyclops the Submarine Captain

#48 Davy Cockett

#49 Dick Danger
the One-Eyed Ranger

#50 Dick Tracy

#51 Dirty Stick

#52 Donkey Dong

#53 Donut Holder

#54 Dr. Feelgood

#55 Dribbling Dart of Love

#56 Eggplant Parma Johnson

#57 Elmer Pudd

#58 Everlasting Gob Dropper

#59 Fire-Breathing Dragon

#60 Flesh Submarine

#61 Skin Winnebago

#65 Fuck Puppet

#66 Fudge Packer
#67 Giggle Stick

#68 Hairy Houdini

#69 Ham and Eggs

#70 Hairy and The Hendersons

#71 Heat-Seeking Moisture Missle

#72
Helmet Head

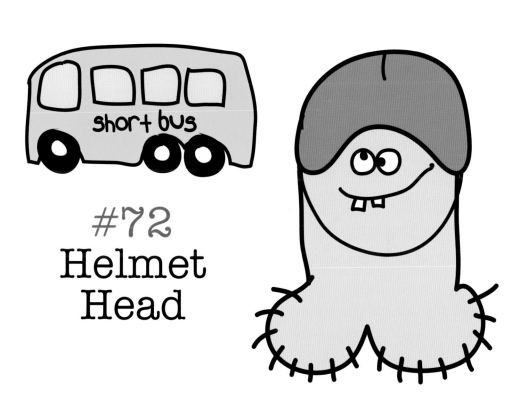

#73 Herman Munster

#74 Hickory Dickory Cock

#75 Honk the Magic Goose

HONK!

#76 Hot Beef Injection

#77 Inch Worm

#78 Jack in the Box

#79 Jack the Beanstalk

#85 Komodo Dragon
#86 Kosher Pickle

#87 Leaky Faucet

#88 Leaning Tower of Penis

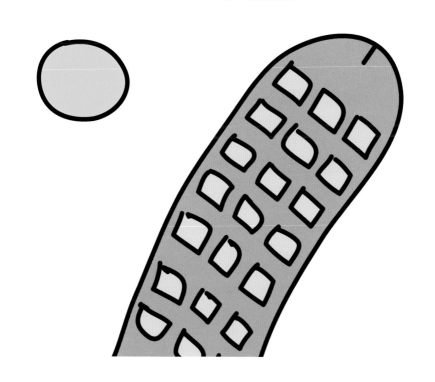

#89 Lip Stick

#90
Big
Dipper

#91 Little Meat Engine
That Could

#92 Lizard with a Saggy Chin

#93 Log of Love

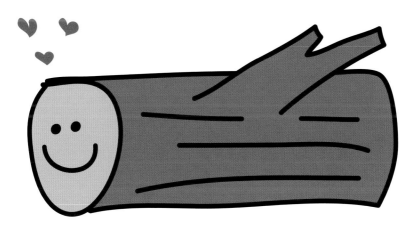

#94 Louisville Plugger

#95 Lunchwagon

#96 Magic Johnson

#97
Mayonnaise Meatloaf

#98 McLovin"

#99 Meat-n-Potatoes

#100 Meat Tampon

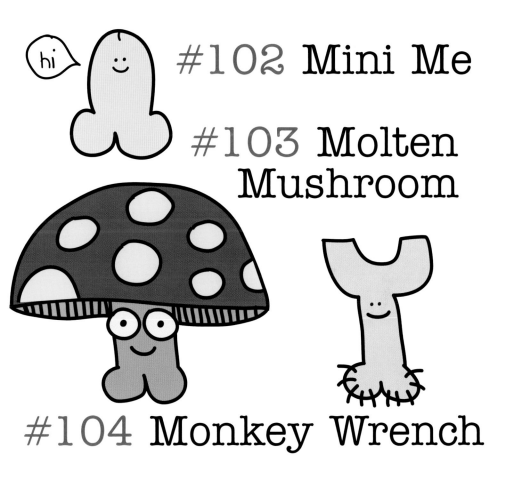

#105 Mr. Belvedere

#106 Mr. Bigglesworth

#107 Mr. Grumpy

#108 Mr. Happy

#109 Mr. Potato Head

#113 Nuts and Bolt

#114 Officer Friendly

#115 Old Faithful

#116 One-Eyed Bathtub Eel

#117 One-Eyed Wonder Worm

#118 One-Holed Bologna Phone

#119 Oscar Meyer Weiner

NICE BUNS

#120 Otis Deepthroatis

#121 Panty Dropper

#124 Peanut Butter and Jism

#125 Penis the Menace

#126 Pig Sticker

#127 Pink Cadillac

#128 Pink Flamingo

#129 Pink Jesus

#130 Plymouth Cock

#131 Polish Sausage
#132 Poon Farmer

#133 Porksicle
#134 Porky Pig

#135 Prince Charming

#136 Protein Shake

#137 Protein Spigot

#138 Pudding Pop
#139 Puds McKenzie

#140 Pump-Action Porridge Bazooka

#141 Purple-Headed Custard Chucker

#142 Purple-Helmeted Spartan of Love

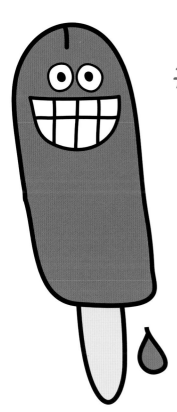

#143 Purple Popsicle

#144 Purple-Veined Midget Muncher

#145 Pussy Plumber

Say NO to crack!

#146 Quarter Pounder

#147 Ralph the Fur-Faced chicken

#148 Red-Headed Step Child

#149 Richard Dickson

#150 Riding Lawn Mower

john speere

zzz!

#151 Rip Van Wrinkle

#152 Rump Wrangler

#153 Rumple Foreskin

#154 Russell the
Love Mussel

#155 Salty Dog

#156 Santa's Little Helper

#157 Sasquatch
#158 Semen Sailor

#159 Sex Pistol
#160 Shiny Banana

#161 Shrimp Boat Captain

#162
Single-Serving
Soup Dispenser

#163
Sir Spanks
A Lot

#164 Skin Flute

#165 Slide Trombone

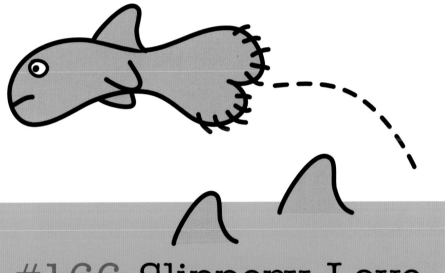

#166 Slippery Love Dolphin

#167 Sludge Pump

#168 Snail Trail Blazer

#169 Snapper Slapper

#170 Snot Sausage

Ah Chooo!

#171
Spackle
Hammer

#172 Sperminator

I'LL BE BACK!

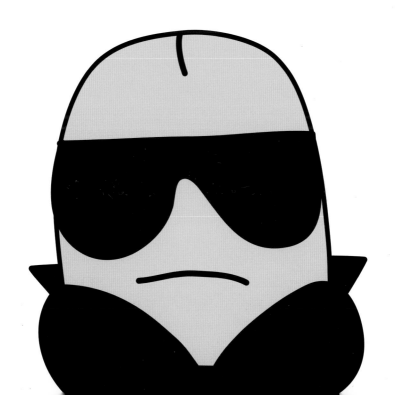

#173 Spunky Monkey

#174 Spiffy Stiffy

#175
Squirmin' Herman the One-Eyed German

#176 Squirt Gun

#177 Stick of Butter

#178 Stick of Dynomite

#179 Stocking Stuffer

#180
Super
Soaker

MOM

#181
Sushi Roll

#182 Sword Fighter

#183 Tallywhacker

#184 Tennessee Throatwarmer

#185 The Bee Hive

#186 The Devirginator

#187 The Ice Cream Maker

#188 The Incredible Bulk

#189 The Love Boat

#190 The Naughty Manatee

#191 The Other White Meat

#192 The Titanic

#193 The Spoo Fighter

#194 The Wonder From Down Under

#195 Three's Company

#196 Thunder Stick

#197 Tickle Me Elmo

#198 Tiddlywinker

#199 Tinky Winky

#200 Tiny Tim

#201 Tonsil Toothbrush

#202 Tootsie Roll

#203
Toy for Twats

#204 Train
Conductor

#205
Trouser
Trolley

#206
Tube Steak

#207 Tuna
Helper

#208
Tuna Troller

#209 Turkey Baster

#210 Turkey Neck

#211 Turtle Head

#212
Ugly Stick

#213 Uncle Throbby
#214 Unicorn Wrangler

#215 Vagina Ninja

#216 Valedicktorian

#217 Walrus Meat

#218 Waxy Meatloaf

#219 Weapon of Ass Destruction

#220
Wet Willy

#221 Wet Whistle Stick

#222 Whatchootalkin About Willy?

#223 Willie Nelson

#224 Willy Wonka and the Chocolate Factory

#225 Winky the Tunnel Ferret

#226 The Wizard of Oz

#227 Wonder Bread

#228 Wonder Wand

#229 Woody Woodpecker

#230 Woody Harrelson

#231 Wooly Mammoth

#232 Wrinkle-Neck Trouser Trout

#233 Wrinkly Devil

#234 Yogurt Slinger

#235 YOU!

DON'T BE A DICK
MEASURE YOUR STICK

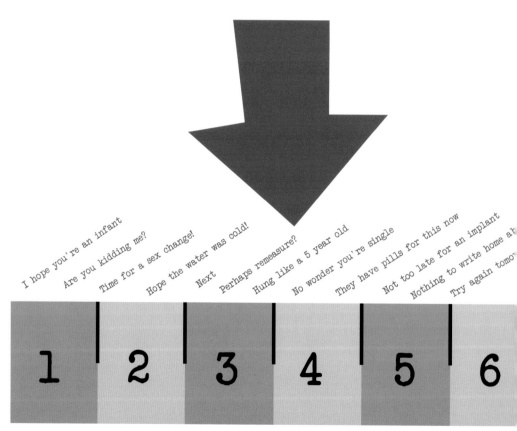

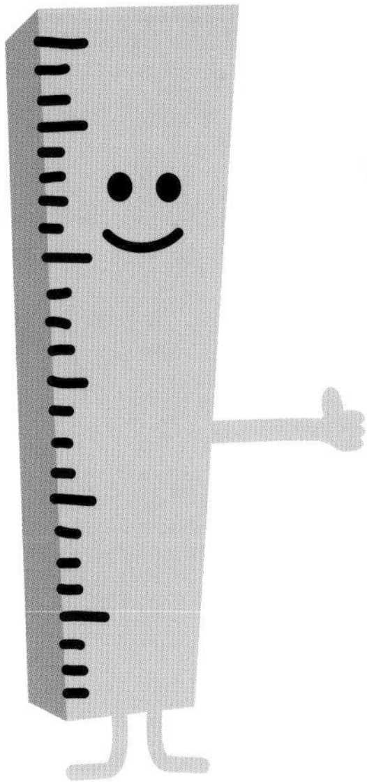

IT'S OK TO CHEAT WHEN NO ONE'S LOOKING!

Instructions:

1. unzip.
2. measure.
3. add 2 inches.
4. brag to your friends.

ok to be average

Your grandfather would be proud

Hi five

Better than most

We're not in Kansas anymore

Now we're talking

Wow!

Is your dad a donkey?

Can you say porn star?

Holy smokes!

You might not be human

You belong in a barn

Ouch!

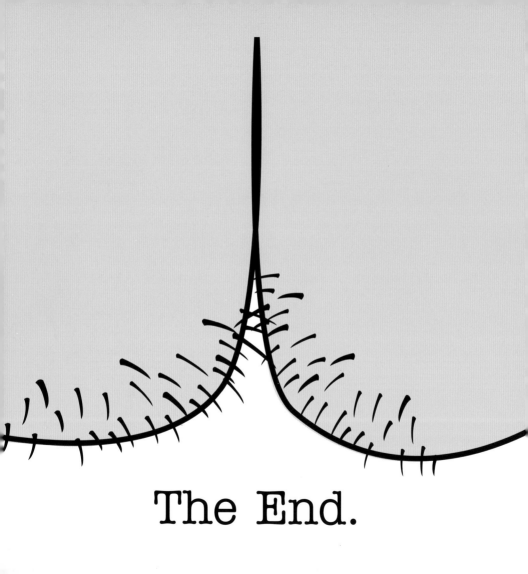

The End.